erstar Cars

Corvette

Lynn Peppas

Superstar Cars

Author: Lynn Peppas
Publishing plan research and development: Sean Charlebois, Reagan Miller Crabtree Publishing Company
Editor: Sonya Newland
Proofreader: Molly Aloian
Editorial director: Kathy Middleton
Project coordinator and prepress technician: Margaret Salter
Print coordinator: Katherine Berti
Series consultant: Petrina Gentile
Cover design: Ken Wright
Design: Simon Borrough
Photo research: Amy Sparks

Photographs:
Alamy: Transtock Inc.: p. 11, 12, 14, 26–27, 46, 48–49, 50; Oleksiy Maksymenko: p. 13; Performance Image: p. 17; www.white-windmill.co.uk: pp. 24–25; imagebroker: p. 25; Phil Talbot: p. 28; culture-images GmbH: p. 45; Retouch UK: p. 55; Drive Images: p. 58
Corbis: Michael Ochs Archives: p. 6; Car Culture: p. 8; Bettmann: p. 9; Robert Genat/Transtock: p. 20; Lucas Jackson/Reuters: p. 54
Dreamstime: Richard Lowthian: p. 1, 21; Patrick Allen: p. 31; Dana Johnson: p. 41; Nomapu: pp. 52–53; Folco Banfi: p. 56–57.
GM Photostore: p. 7, 10, 18, 19, 26, 29, 30, 32–33, 34–35, 35, 36, 37, 39, 40, 43, 44, 59
Motoring Picture Library: p. 4, 14–15, 16, 22, 23, 38, 51.
Shutterstock: front cover; Dongliu: p. 4–5; Stephen Hew: p. 42; Boykov: p. 47; KSPhotography: p. 48

Library and Archives Canada Cataloguing in Publication

Peppas, Lynn
Corvette / Lynn Peppas.

(Superstar cars)
Includes index.
Issued also in an electronic format.
ISBN 978-0-7787-2141-3 (bound).--ISBN 978-0-7787-2148-2 (pbk.)

1. Corvette automobile--Juvenile literature.
I. Title. II. Series: Superstar cars

TL215.C67P46 2011 j629.222'2 C2010-905626-4

Library of Congress Cataloging-in-Publication Data

Peppas, Lynn.
Corvette / Lynn Peppas.
p. cm. -- (Superstar cars)
Includes index.
ISBN 978-0-7787-2148-2 (pbk. : alk. paper) --
ISBN 978-0-7787-2141-3 (reinforced library binding : alk. paper) --
ISBN 978-1-4271-9546-3 (electronic (pdf))
1. Corvette automobile--Juvenile literature. I. Title. II. Series.

TL215.C6P39 2010
629.222'2--dc22

2010034933

Crabtree Publishing Company

Printed in the U.S.A./102010/SP20100915

www.crabtreebooks.com 1-800-387-7650
 In Canada: We acknowledge the financial support of the Government of Canada through the Canada Book Fund for our publishing activities.

Published in Canada
Crabtree Publishing
616 Welland Ave.
St. Catharines, ON
L2M 5V6

Published in the United States
Crabtree Publishing
PMB 59051
350 Fifth Avenue, 59th Floor
New York, New York 10118

Published in the United Kingdom
Crabtree Publishing
Maritime House
Basin Road North, Hove
BN41 1WR

Published in Australia
Crabtree Publishing
386 Mt. Alexander Rd.
Ascot Vale (Melbourne)
VIC 3032

Contents

Chapter 1

America's First Sports Car

The Corvette has been called "America's favorite sports car" for many years now—by car enthusiasts and drivers alike. This may sound like an exaggeration, but any car that's pushing 60 years old and still looks this good deserves such a title!

That's a Corvette...

Corvette also has the distinction of being America's oldest **production** sports car. But through the years and through all the design changes, the car has maintained a look that says, "that's a Corvette," right away. It has always looked sleek, lean, and low-to-the-ground—and has led the way in American sports-car design. Add "fastest American production sports car" to the list, too. The icing on the cake is that Corvette prides itself on being one of the most affordable high-performance vehicles, especially when compared with some of its European competitors.

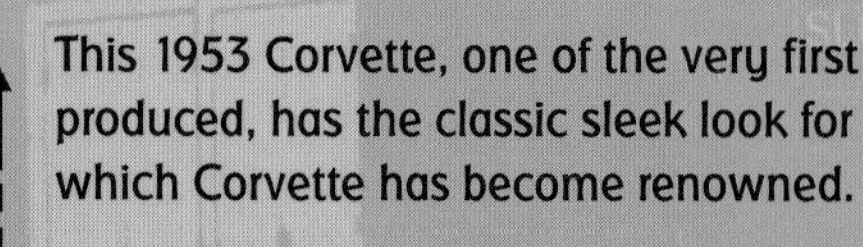

This 1953 Corvette, one of the very first produced, has the classic sleek look for which Corvette has become renowned.

A work of art

For over half a century, the Corvette has been an American work of art on wheels—as amazing to look at as to drive. Best of all, the Corvette has always been fairly priced. These factors have combined to make it a favorite with both Americans and many other car enthusiasts from all over the world.

GM: Big Three automaker

Corvette is made by General Motors (GM), one of the so-called Big Three U.S. automakers. GM has several divisions, including Chevrolet, Cadillac, and GMC. Corvette is the sports car produced by the Chevrolet division. Although GM does make cars and parts in some other countries, the Corvette is made in the United States.

Nearly 60 years on, Corvettes are still icons of American style in motoring.

What's in a name?

Say the word "Corvette" today, and people everywhere automatically think of the sports car. But say that same word in the early 1950s—just five years after World War II ended—and people would have thought of a fast-moving warship instead. In 1953, General Motors wanted the name of its new sports car to start with the letter C, but they didn't want to name it after an animal, which was what many other companies did.

A GM employee named Myron Scott had been reading about the corvette, a small, fast escort ship. Myron sent a note to the chief engineer at GM, Ed Cole, and suggested the name "Corvette" for the new car. Ed loved it. The vehicle has been called Corvette ever since, although many people often shorten it to its popular nickname, 'Vette.

The Corvette became an icon in the 1960s, sung about by popular groups such as The Beach Boys.

Something to sing about

Musicians worldwide have cashed in on the fact that everybody knows about the racy Corvette image. Singers such as the Beach Boys in "Shut Down," George Jones in "Corvette Song," Prince in "Little Red Corvette," and Eiffel 65 in "I'm Blue" all sing about the Corvette in their song lyrics.

Corvettes don't just look good on the outside—beneath the shell, every detail is carefully planned and engineered.

Just a pretty face?

Some people say that beauty is only skin deep. It's true that the Corvette's "skin" is beautiful, but besides its great look, this sports car has a lot of character in terms of **state-of-the-art** technology and engineering. Behind every model, there are a lot of people who have worked hard to make the car what it is.

The people behind the car

GM has always employed a special team of the very best carmakers, including people who design, engineer, market, and produce Corvette models that are consistently top in their class.

Corvette teamwork

Designers are the people who think up the style and look of a car. The engineers work on a car's performance—making sure it will run efficiently and smoothly. Marketers make up the creative team that thinks of ways to sell more cars to the public. When all this work is done, the production people are responsible for actually putting the car together on the assembly lines in GM's factories and plants.

Altogether, the teams that create Corvettes have put out some of the most unforgettable—and collectible—sports cars in America.

Chapter 2

The American Dream Car

The 1950s was a decade of great change. Many Americans had had enough of sadness and struggle after the long years of World War II. They were ready to enjoy themselves. As the economy recovered, people began to have more money to spend on items such as cars, too.

Life in the 1950s

In the early 1950s, technology was not what it is today. Cars did not have seat belts. Television had just started to make its way into average Americans' homes. Though the first color television came out in 1951, most people lucky enough to own a set had a black-and-white one. Airlines began using jet planes for passenger flights only in the late 1950s.

In the early 1950s, the Chevrolet division of General Motors, which had mainly produced sedans, decided to add a sports car to its collection.

Rebirth of an industry

Before the 1950s, American car buyers had very little choice when it came to style or color in their automobiles. That all changed after 1949, when vehicles were given special names (other than **sedan**), modern styles, and colors. It was an exciting time in many ways, but especially in the automotive industry.

GM looks forward

General Motors felt it was time to create the first two-seater, American-style sports car. Most sports cars on American roads were imported from European automakers, and GM wanted to show the world that American automakers could keep up with the best of them. They created a sports car that was fun to look at—and to drive. They called it EX-122. Today, we call it the Corvette.

Fiberglass class

In 1953, car bodies were made of steel, and in fact most still are today. One of the unique features of the 1953 Corvette was that it was made from a material no other production car had been made of before—fiberglass. Chevrolet built one of its first Corvette test cars in fiberglass. Engineers found it weighed about 200 pounds (91 kg) less than a car body made of steel. During driving tests, the fiberglass body was found to be very sturdy, too.

AMAZING FACTS

Light but strong

Fiberglass is made from glass fibers surrounded by a liquid plastic. When heated, the mixture can be poured into a mold of a particular shape. When it cools it hardens. Fiberglass is very strong and lightweight compared to steel and does not rust like steel.

The first Corvettes roll off the production line in Flint, Michigan. GM decided that fiberglass was the best material for the bodies.

Body building

In 1953, Chevrolet ordered fiberglass body parts for its first production Corvettes. Altogether there were 62 fiberglass parts to be glued together to form the outer body. There were times when GM thought about making Corvettes with steel bodies instead, but they came to fully appreciate the many benefits of fiberglass car bodies. Corvettes are still made of fiberglass today.

Dream car a reality

Chevrolet decided to start production on 300 new Corvettes in June 1953. The company's aim was to produce a stylish sports car with good performance and luxurious comfort. They also wanted to keep the price tag as low as possible. To do this, engineers used as many parts as they could from other Chevrolet cars for the Corvette. Recycled Chevrolet parts that were used on the Corvette included steering and braking systems and a basic engine called the Blue Flame "straight-six."

Motorama dream car

The first concept Corvette made its first public appearance at a Motorama car show held at the Waldorf Astoria Hotel in New York City, on January 17, 1953. GM held Motorama car shows at major cities in the United States to see if people were interested in their new *concept cars*. Almost everyone had the same response to the new Corvette—they loved it!

The 1953 Corvette went on display at the Motorama show in New York. The car later went into production with very few changes to its styling.

Some Chevrolet parts, such as the straight-six engine, were upgraded for the Corvette. "Straight-six" referred to the straight-line arrangement of the six cylinders.

Low-slung chassis

A low-to-the-ground **chassis** was one of the new features of the Corvette. The car sat so low, in fact, that the roofline was only 47 inches (119 cm) high. The design costs pushed the price for the Corvette higher than Chevrolet had planned. Instead of the targeted US$2,000 price tag, the Corvette would now cost more than US$3,000. This may not sound like a lot of money, but back in 1953, US$3,000 was worth over US$24,000 today.

First off the line

The very first production Corvette came off the assembly line at Chevrolet's Flint, Michigan, plant on June 30, 1953. Building the first production Corvette was a long, drawn-out process to begin with. Carmakers were learning how to work with fiberglass as they went. The first car had taken a crew of carmakers six eight-hour shifts to make.

Production of Corvettes became faster, and by August 1953, Chevrolet was building three Corvettes a day. This was still much more time than it took to build other assembly-line produced Chevrolet cars, though.

1953 Corvettes

The entire production run of 1953 Corvettes—all 300 of them—looked exactly the same. They had polo white exteriors with smart red interiors. Every one had a black canvas convertible top and **whitewall tires**. The reason for this was to keep production as smooth as possible. The workers on the assembly line had enough to concentrate on without worrying about matching trim and body color.

The first Corvette was classified as a **roadster**—an open-body vehicle. The convertible roof was not power-operated. It had to be taken down by hand, folded, and placed into the storage compartment behind the seats.

AMAZING FACTS

Double-O-Three Corvette

The third-ever Corvette is the oldest production Corvette known to exist today. It is called the Double-O-Three because the last three digits of its production number were 003. The first two Corvettes off the assembly line were used as test cars and eventually destroyed.

All 1953 Corvettes had red and white interior features and upholstery. The exterior paintwork was polo white.

The 1953 Corvette had recessed headlights. One notable design feature was the steel wire-mask that covered these lights.

Design features

The 1953 Corvette featured a wraparound windshield—a design style copied from an aircraft. This was the only window on the vehicle. Instead of glass roll-up side windows, it had removable plastic ones. The car did not have door handles on the outer body, either. The driver or passenger had to reach inside to open the door.

The first production Corvette had **recessed** headlights set flush with the body of the car. This headlight style is one of the key similarities between all Corvettes.

Harley Earl

Harley Earl is sometimes called the Father of the Corvette. He worked at GM as chief designer and convinced company executives to create the two-seater sports car. He was a man of many firsts. He was the first designer to use clay instead of wood when designing all models of cars. He was the first to design a car with a wraparound windshield. The GM Motorama car show was his idea, too!

Less than dreamy

The 1953 Corvette could not be purchased by just anybody. Instead, GM decided that some would be offered to celebrities—such as the actor John Wayne. Others were given to large dealerships with showrooms that could display the models. The idea was to create a buzz about the Corvette first and then rack up the sales later.

Later in 1953, when the Corvette finally went on sale to the public, it was not the hit that GM had expected. Part of the problem may have been that early production cars' fiberglass panels had not been fitted together properly, and there were gaps and leaks where there shouldn't have been.

1953 Corvette

Production years: 1953
No. built: 300
Top speed: 105 mph (169 km/h)
Engine type: Blue Flame straight-6
Engine size: 235.5 ci (3.85 liter), 150 hp
Cylinders: 6
Transmission: 2-speed automatic Powerglide
CO_2 emissions: N/A
EPA fuel economy ratings: N/A
Price: US$3,498

The early Corvettes had automatic transmission, which many people felt did not give the driver the handling required for a sports car.

Performance problems

Performance-wise there were problems, too. Many people did not like the **automatic transmission** and felt a sports car should have a **manual transmission** instead. Even though the Corvette was considered fast, some family cars could still travel faster. Still, any brand new production car is going to experience some wrinkles that need to be ironed out. Considering the speed of production and the brand-new fiberglass body material—which few people were familiar with—the Corvette did very well in its first year.

The first production Corvette could go from 0 to 60 mph (97 km/h) in 11 seconds.

Chapter 3

Corvette's First 30 Years

The Corvette's first three years in production were rocky to say the least, and these problems resulted in poor sales. Chevrolet had hoped Corvette would sell many more cars than it did between 1953 and 1955. In 1954, over 3,600 Corvettes were made. The number dropped to 700 the following year. Chevrolet designers and engineers worked hard to get the Corvette up to speed—and up in sales.

A poor start

In an effort to boost sales, in 1954, Chevrolet offered four colors to choose from, and cut the price by about US$500, which would be a saving of about US$4,000 today. In 1955, the company added the option for a faster engine. Still, the cars did not sell well and GM executives talked about discontinuing production of the Corvette.

Some GM employees, such as engineer Zora Arkus-Duntov, designer Bill Mitchell, and engineer Ed Cole, went to bat for the car they loved so much.

Corvette moves to St. Louis

Only the 1953 Corvettes were made in the factory at Flint, Michigan. In 1954, production moved to GM's plant in St. Louis, Missouri. Here, workers could produce up to 1,000 Corvettes a month. Corvettes were made in St. Louis for 27 years—until 1981, when production was moved to the current Bowling Green, Kentucky, plant.

The 1954 Corvette was offered in more than just polo white—but other than this it looked just like the 1953 model.

Although the V8 engine was offered in the 1955 model, the first seven off the production line still had the old Blue Flame engine.

Keeping the Corvette

In the end they convinced GM to keep the Corvette. It was a good thing they did—years of hard work and expertise eventually made the Corvette the most talked-about sports car in the world. When the car finally caught on, almost the entire nation had Corvette fever.

Fixing the problems

Engineers worked on fixing the Corvette's performance. They gave the 1955 model a new V8 small-block engine, which ramped up the speed of the car—one of the main complaints about the earlier models. Even though the Corvette performed much better in 1955 than it had up to that point, the problem was that it looked almost exactly the same as the 1953 model. What it needed was a new look that matched its new performance standards.

A new look

The new look was unveiled in 1956. The 1956 model is sometimes called the "real McCoy." This means that it was what Corvette should have been all along—in other words, it was the "real thing."

The 1956 model had two new features that earlier Corvettes had often been criticized for not having. These were roll-up glass windows, and a door handle on the car's exterior. Even though all Corvettes were designed as convertibles, a removable hardtop could also be purchased. These were all big changes to the Corvette—but change didn't stop there!

Corvette Club of America

The Corvette Club of America (CCA) was founded in 1956. It is the oldest Corvette club in the world. The club hosts car shows, races, and social events. In order to be a member of the CCA, you have to own a Corvette and pay a membership fee. The club's headquarters are situated in Gaithersburg, Maryland.

The fortunes of Corvette really changed with the introduction of the new-look model in 1956.

1956 Corvette

Production years: 1956–57
No. built: 3,467
Top speed: 118 mph (190 km/h)
Engine type: Small-block V8
Engine size: 265 ci (4.34 liter), 225 hp
Cylinders: 8
Transmission: 3-speed manual (standard); 2-speed automatic (optional)
CO_2 emissions: N/A
EPA fuel economy ratings: N/A
Price: US$2,900

In 1956, all Corvettes were equipped with a V8 small-block engine. The car could do 0 to 60 mph (97 km/h) in 7.3 seconds.

Light changes

The front headlight and rear taillight detail was almost completely reversed from the earlier models. The headlights were changed from being recessed within the body to being mounted on front fender wings. The distinctive metal-cage coverings were discontinued and were replaced with glass. Taillights were recessed within the curved rear end of the car.

Magical makeover

Another big style change was seen in the side **coves**, which started behind the front wheel and ended at almost the length of the door. In 1956, these coves were painted white. The front hood was also designed with curvy bulges—making it look like it was bursting with power. This feature remained a part of the **signature** look of the Corvette for many years.

Corvette evolution

The 1956 Corvette's style changes increased sales dramatically. After that, Corvette didn't stop evolving and every year brought some kind of change—some large and others small. In 1957, Arkus-Duntov and his team of engineers introduced the first fuel-injected engine to the Corvette. In fact, this was the first fuel-injected motor in any American-built car. It was one of the biggest changes in terms of performance, adding more speed to the car.

1958 Corvette

Styling changes in 1958 included the installation of a pair of headlights on both sides instead of just one. Chrome was coming into car fashion, and the 1958 Corvette sported three chrome strips inside the side coves. More and more chrome additions were added during the next three years. The chrome made the Corvette much heavier.

End of a generation

Although the first-generation Corvette struggled at the start, it was a winner by the time it went out of production. Even today its classic design and spirited performance make it one of the most collectible and sought-after generations of Corvette.

Chrome was becoming very fashionable for cars in the late 1950s. More chrome details were added to the 1958 Corvette.

Corvette generations

Most models of cars are produced for about ten years and then are either discontinued or replaced with different models. Not many have been around for as long as the Corvette, which has been coming off the assembly line for over 50 years. Throughout that time there have been many changes in style and performance. For this reason, Corvettes are classified into generations.

There are six generations of Corvette. The generation is written with a capital C followed by a number. C1s are the original Corvettes, built from 1953 to 1962. C1s are often called the "solid-axle" generation because all their back axles are one piece. C2s were built from 1963 to 1967, C3s from 1968 to 1982, C4s from 1984 to 1996, C5s from 1997 to 2004, and C6s since 2005.

1962 Corvette

Production years: 1962
No. built: 14,531
Top speed: 150 mph (241 km/h)
Engine type: Small-block V8
Engine size: 327 ci (5.35 liter), 360 hp
Cylinders: 8
Transmission: 3-speed manual (standard); 2-speed Powerglide automatic or 4-speed manual (optional)
CO_2 emissions: N/A
EPA fuel economy ratings: N/A
Price: US$4,038

The 1962 model marked the end of the first generation of Corvette. The small-block V8 engine was made even bigger. It could now do 0 to 60 mph (97 km/h) in 5.9 seconds.

Hidden headlamps and a new, angular body shape were just two of the revolutionary design changes that were given to the 1963 Corvette.

Ringing the changes

The first-generation Corvette design lasted for nine years. GM decided that for the 1963 model it was time for a change. **Maverick** car designer Bill Mitchell had recently been made chief of design at GM, and he had very different ideas about how the new generation of Corvette should look. The first-generation body had sloping, rounded lines. Under Bill's direction the second generation looked quite the opposite, with edges and angles instead. The car was also given a new name—Sting Ray.

Inner luxury

Inside the 1963 Corvette, luxury items such as power steering, air conditioning, and leather seats were available for the first time. Another first was that it came in two separate body styles: the convertible or fastback Sport **coupe**.

Outer style

Another improvement for the 1963 Corvette was the **retractable**, or hidden, headlights. Arkus-Duntov and his team used electric motors to operate them. Hidden headlights remained a Corvette signature design for many years—until the sixth generation, in fact.

The most talked-about change in design was the rear window, which was split with a divider. This feature was only found in the 1963 Sport coupe. The split back window had largely been Mitchell's idea, and other GM employees had argued against it. They thought that it created vision problems when drivers looked out the back. This divided window was replaced with a single window the following year.

Improved performance

As far as performance went, thanks to Arkus-Duntov and his engineering team, the second generation was better than ever in terms of steering and handling. It now had a newly designed chassis that cut four inches (ten cm) off the wheelbase, and weighed less. Also new was the independent rear suspension (IRS) instead of the solid axle characteristic of the first generation. The rear wheels were on two drive shafts, with joints that allowed them to move separately from one another.

Rare Sting Ray

Many 1963 Sport Corvette owners disliked the divided back windows. Some took them to custom workshops and replaced them with single glass windows. Just try to find a mint split-window model today! They are a rare breed indeed, and this makes them very valuable.

The split back window was one of the most talked-about design changes that appeared on the 1963 Corvette.

Muscle-car mania

Interest in **muscle-cars** was a popular trend that began in the 1960s. A muscle car is simply a small car with a big engine. Unlike a sports car, a muscle car could be a four-seater—in fact it could be any car, as long as it had a ridiculously large engine and could travel at lightning-quick speeds!

The big-block

Cars that Corvette had easily left in the dust suddenly began to sport larger engines and take the lead. Chevrolet couldn't let that happen. The answer was to up the **horsepower** in the Corvette's engines. The big-block V8 became an engine option available for Corvette muscle-car enthusiasts in 1965. The addition of a side exhaust pipe in 1965 made it look more muscular, too.

Vital Statistics

1966 Corvette

Production years: 1966
No. built: 27,720
Top speed: 135 mph (217 km/h)
Engine type: Small-block V8
Engine size: 327 ci (5.35 liter), 300 hp
Cylinders: 8
Transmission: 3-speed manual; automatic or 4-speed manual (optional)
CO_2 emissions: N/A
EPA fuel economy ratings: N/A
Price: US$4,295

Small-block and big-block

The difference between small-block and big-block engines is in their size. Both engines run on eight cylinders arranged in a V shape. Small-blocks have smaller pistons and bores, and the piston strokes are shorter; they are smaller overall. Big-blocks have larger pistons and bores and longer strokes; thus, they are larger. They are also more powerful.

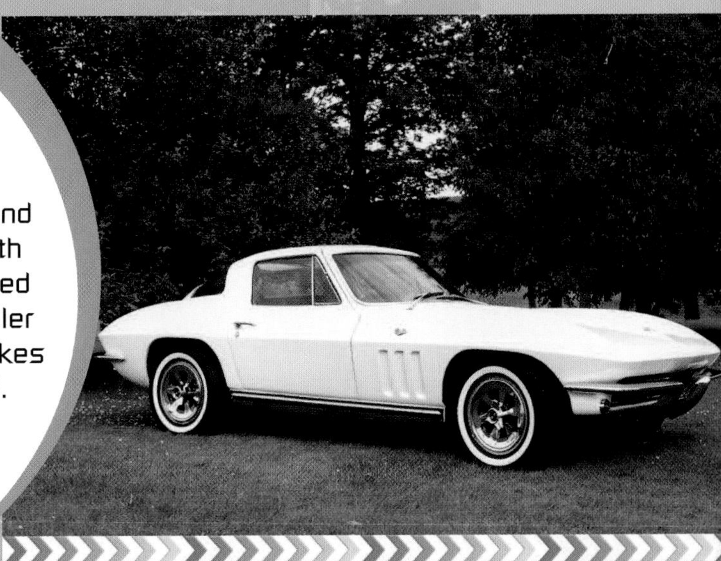

With a standard small-block V8 engine under the hood, the 1966 'Vette could do 0 to 60 mph (97 km/h) in 5.6 seconds.

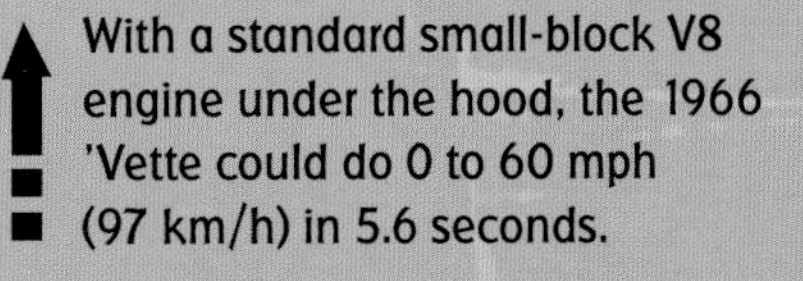

For the first time, with the 1965 Sting Ray, Corvette entered the muscle-car race with a big-block engine option.

Speed and power

American drivers became obsessed with speed in terms of horsepower. Many muscle cars could travel in a straight line at top speeds, but they weren't equipped with proper steering, handling, or braking systems.

The Corvette could not only bring out the power—it could handle it, too, when driving the curves and stops of an average American road. This is where it had an obvious advantage. In 1966, the first 427 ci big-block engine was introduced. Like most trends, the obsession with speed and power came and then went as the 1960s turned into the 1970s, and as concern about the environment became a factor.

The third generation

Corvettes were riding high on their reputation for being the complete package. The cars went remarkably fast, handled remarkably well, and did it all with remarkable style. Mitchell was confident that a new body design in 1968 would push the Corvette into superstardom. He was absolutely correct. The C3 generation had the longest production run with the most Corvette's produced.

The third generation (C3) of Corvettes was launched in 1968—again with extreme changes in its design features and cutting-edge technologies for the day.

A sporty new look

The coupe had a two-piece, T-top roof that remained for all third-generation Corvettes. The side vent windows that had been characteristic since 1956 were removed and replaced with a single glass window. The traditional rounded bar door handles had been replaced with sporty push-button door openers instead. The back window was changed from a sloping fastback to a vertical scoop style that was removable. A soft-top convertible was also available. The shortened, choppier rear end still kept the signature double taillights on each side.

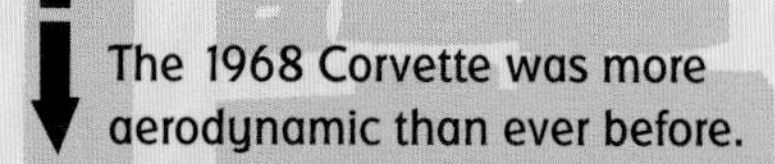

The 1968 Corvette was more aerodynamic than ever before.

The Mako Shark

Mitchell and another designer, Larry Shinoda, came up with a production design for Corvette based on an earlier concept car called the Mako Shark (see page 48). The changes to the Corvette body shape were very different from the earlier C2 Sting Ray. C3 Corvettes had curvy, rounded front and rear fenders that tapered down into a slimmer waistline around the seating area.

Aerodynamics

Arkus-Duntov and his engineering team made sure that the new design was the most **aerodynamic** Corvette yet, thanks to the many tests he ran on it. This meant it provided the least wind resistance when traveling and had less **drag**. The earlier Sting Ray was much less aerodynamic. At high speeds the body tended to lift up and create wind resistance, which slowed the vehicle.

Optical instruments

Another change was the use of fiber optics in the instrument panel. Fiber optics are long, thin strands of glass that carry light signals to their ends. This was state-of-the-art technology for 1968.

Clean Air Act

In 1963, the U.S. Congress passed the Clean Air Act, a law aimed at controlling air pollution. In 1970, another antipollution law was enacted; it required that all new cars produced by 1975 must cut their **emissions** by 90 percent. From 1975 onward, all Corvette engines came equipped with a **catalytic converter** that cut emissions and ran on unleaded gas only.

Powerhouse secret

The third generation of Corvette still offered buyers a variety of big-block engine options up until 1975. Its best-kept secret was the L88 engine. L88 was a big-block, with 427 ci (seven-liter) displacement and a single Holley four-barrel carburetor. It was first offered from 1967 to 1969. For all three years, only 218 Corvettes with this engine were ever sold.

The 1969 model had some minor changes, including a smaller steering wheel and an ignition switch on the steering column rather than the dash.

High octane!

Dealers discouraged the public from buying the L88 edition cars. They did not come with air conditioning or radios. They ran on higher-octane racing gas that not all gas stations carried. All this meant was that a Corvette equipped with an L88 engine could go fast—extremely fast. It could travel at top speeds of 170 mph (273 km/h). It certainly wasn't a car for the average around-town driver.

AMAZING FACTS

Stingray

The third-generation Corvette's first production car, the 1968 model, was not given the Sting Ray name. The name was brought back again for the 1969 model but the spelling had been changed from two words—Sting Ray—to just one word, Stingray.

Third-generation changes

The third generation was the longest-lasting generation of Corvette to this day. The design lasted for 14 years. Throughout this time, changes were made—some large and some small—to different models within the generation's life span.

Plastic pieces

Chrome—once so popular—was slowly falling out of fashion. The 1973 model was the first to have a front bumper with no chrome on it at all. The new nose was made entirely out of **urethane plastic**. It was made to meet the new U.S. government safety standards. Chrome disappeared off the rear bumper the following year (1974) and was replaced by the same urethane material. By 1978, all chrome had disappeared except for the pushdown door handles and key locks.

"Corvette Summer"

American actor Mark Hamill (who had starred a year earlier as Luke Skywalker in the movie "Star Wars") also appeared in a 1978 theater-released movie called "Corvette Summer." The film tells the story of a high-school boy who helps work on a Corvette as a shop project. When the car is stolen he spends his summer searching for it.

The 1973 Corvette had a new nose treatment. The chrome bumper was replaced with a plastic one.

Environmental concerns

By the mid-1970s, people were less interested in an engine's horsepower and speed and more concerned about the environment. Early third-generation Corvettes—from 1968 to 1974—could be purchased with optional big-block engines, but they too were extinct by 1975. They simply could not pass the new emissions standards.

Engineers went back to work on the small-block V8 to give it more speed. They achieved this by beefing it up from 327 ci (5.35 liters) to 350 ci (5.7 liters).

Gas-guzzler tax

The Energy Tax Act is a U.S. federal law enacted in 1978. Its object was to help conserve energy. A provision of this act is the gas-guzzler tax. The government sets an mpg (miles per gallon) value that is fuel-efficient for cars. If cars do not meet this value, owners have to pay a special tax when they buy the car. Later Corvette owners have never had to pay this tax; GM made sure that the car always met the standard value.

The 1975 Corvette was the first model to include a catalytic converter for cleaner driving with less harmful emissions.

Corvette goes green

All Corvettes manufactured during or after 1975 were built with a catalytic converter to help reduce toxic emissions released into the air by the car's engine. New federal legislation required that this converter be installed on all new American-made cars. From the 1975 model on, only small-block engines powered Corvettes.

Convertible dropped

By 1975, convertible sales had dropped drastically. In 1975, 38,465 Corvettes came off the assembly line, but only 4,629 of these were convertibles. Most Corvette buyers liked the T-bar roof that was introduced back in 1968. Owners could enjoy the benefit of driving with the top off in much the same way as with a convertible.

Vital Statistics

1982 Corvette

Production years: 1982
No. built: 25,407
Top speed: 123 mph (200 km/h)
Engine type: Small-block V8
Engine size: 350 ci (5.7 liter), 200 hp
Cylinders: 8
Transmission: 3-speed manual Hydra Matic
CO_2 emissions: N/A
EPA fuel economy ratings: N/A
Price: US$18,290

Anniversary Corvette

In 1978, Corvette celebrated its twenty-fifth (silver) anniversary by releasing a special-edition car with two-tone silver metallic/charcoal gray paint. This year also marked the return to the fastback, wraparound window design for all Corvettes produced. This design feature lasted for the remainder of the third generation.

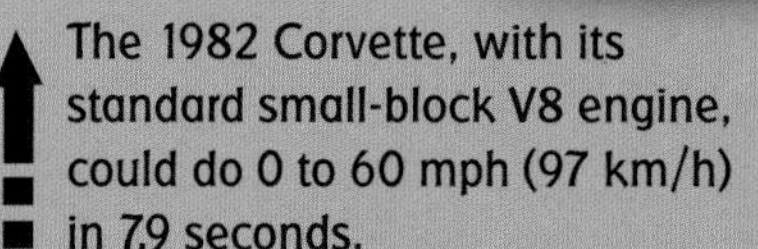

The 1982 Corvette, with its standard small-block V8 engine, could do 0 to 60 mph (97 km/h) in 7.9 seconds.

Chapter 4

The Evolution of Corvette

In the early 1980s, when people talked about the Corvette, they automatically imagined the curvaceous Stingray body, because it had been around for 14 years. Fourteen years for one design is a long time by any standard—but the American public was still loving it. It was sleek, stunning to look at, and fast. What was there not to love?

Looking forward

By 1980, carmakers at GM knew they were overdue for a new design. For the past 30 years they had built the most forward-looking and -driving sports car on American roads. It was time to move into the future with the next generation of Corvette. So, in the next 30 years, GM's Chevrolet division went on to produce three more generations of Corvette. True to its reputation, each generation was considered an American icon of style and performance. A lot was riding on each design, which had to look entirely different—and yet still be recognizable as a Corvette.

AMAZING FACTS

The missing year

In 1983, Corvette reached its thirtieth birthday. Instead of releasing a special 1983 anniversary edition car, though, the company skipped a year—only releasing the 1984 model. There is no such thing as a 1983 Corvette!

Welcome to the eighties

In the early 1980s, the North American economy was in **recession**. Commerce slowed, and many people were having a hard time. Many American businesses were affected, particularly the carmakers. The recession was a result of OPEC's (Organization of Arab Petroleum Exporting Countries) U.S. oil **embargo** in 1973. A second oil crisis in 1979 cut oil **exports** to the U.S. even more.

For North Americans, this meant that the cost of goods went up because oil was so expensive. Many Americans lost their jobs. For the average American, it wasn't a good time to buy a higher-priced luxury sports car.

Facing the competition

American carmakers had another problem—they were losing sales to foreign carmakers. Companies such as Toyota were producing smaller, fuel-efficient cars for American consumers. In 1983 the economy started to recover, and it seemed like the time was right to release a brand-new generation of Corvette.

1984 Corvette

Production years: 1984
No. built: 51,547
Top speed: 140 mph (225 km/h)
Engine type: Small-block V8
Engine size: 350 ci (5.7 liter), 205 hp
Cylinders: 8
Transmission: 4-speed manual or automatic overdrive
CO_2 emissions: 12.4 tons/yr
EPA fuel economy ratings: 14 mpg (city); 22 mpg (highway)
Price: US$21,800

The 1984 Corvette, the first of the fourth generation (C4), could actually be purchased at a Chevrolet dealership on April 21, 1983.

C4 Corvettes

In fact, GM had been at work on a new, fourth-generation (C4) Corvette since 1978. When 1982 came, however, it still wasn't ready. The new model was finally released in the spring of 1983 and officially labeled a 1984.

The C4 Corvette looked like its older Corvette relatives, with hideaway headlights, two round taillights inset in the rear, and side vents behind the front wheels.

The rear glass hatch and one-piece T-roof were new features found on every 1984 Corvette. The new model also had a more aerodynamic design than earlier models.

American beauty

The new shape of the Corvette was aerodynamic, in part because of the design of the windshield, which sat at a remarkably steep 64° angle—the steepest of any production car ever made in America at that time.

The body of the 1984 Corvette was smaller in some ways than its Stingray relative. The C4 was nine inches (22 cm) shorter and over 170 pounds (77 kg) lighter than the 1982 Corvette. It weighed less because heavier parts were replaced with lightweight aluminum and plastic parts. The C4 gained two inches (five cm) in width, which allowed for roomier seating inside—and greater comfort.

Under the hood

The C4 was the first Corvette with a clamshell hood that opened to show off the engine and new aluminum parts. GM went as far as making sculpted handles for the dipsticks; even the battery case was black and gray so it would match its surroundings.

Interior details

Inside, it was a space-age dream. The dashboard was decked out with a then state-of-the-art, all-electronic display that featured LCD (liquid crystal display) and analog readouts. Finally, an antitheft system was installed in every car that left the factory. With those looks and that performance, it would definitely need one!

At the time, the 1984 Corvette was the fastest American production sports car. It could do 0 to 60 mph (97 km/h) in under seven seconds.

Made in the U.S.A.

GM's assembly plant in Bowling Green, Kentucky, is the hometown of all C4, C5, and C6 Corvettes. The plant opened in June of 1981. It was purchased from Chrysler and expanded into a plant of 1,000,000 square feet (93,000 sq m). Today, car owners are invited to watch their Corvettes being built at the plant.

Changes for the C4

The fourth-generation Corvette had a brand new chassis called a uniframe. It was made of steel. The new chassis made the Corvette more rigid and allowed for a single roof panel instead of the two-piece T-top panels. It also made the Corvette a safer car to drive, offering protection if it were involved in a collision.

Car of the Year

The C4's price tag climbed by almost US$3,000. Even with the steep climb in price, though, more people were buying Corvettes than ever before. In 1982, 25,407 Corvettes were sold, but in 1984, the numbers hit 51,547! Only one year of Corvette had ever sold more than that, and that was the 1979 model—which sold 53,807 cars.

By the time the 1986 Corvette coupe model was released, all Corvettes were fitted with ABS as an extra safety feature.

ABS

The C4 Corvettes were the first to have an antilock braking system (ABS). As its name suggests, ABS helps drivers keep control of the vehicle when circumstances require them to hit the brakes hard. Computerized antilock brakes have sensors that can tell when a wheel will lock up. The sensors send a message to a computer, which sends a command to put pressure on the brake but then remove pressure again, so that the brakes are pumped. This lets the driver keep control of the car so that it doesn't skid out and collide.

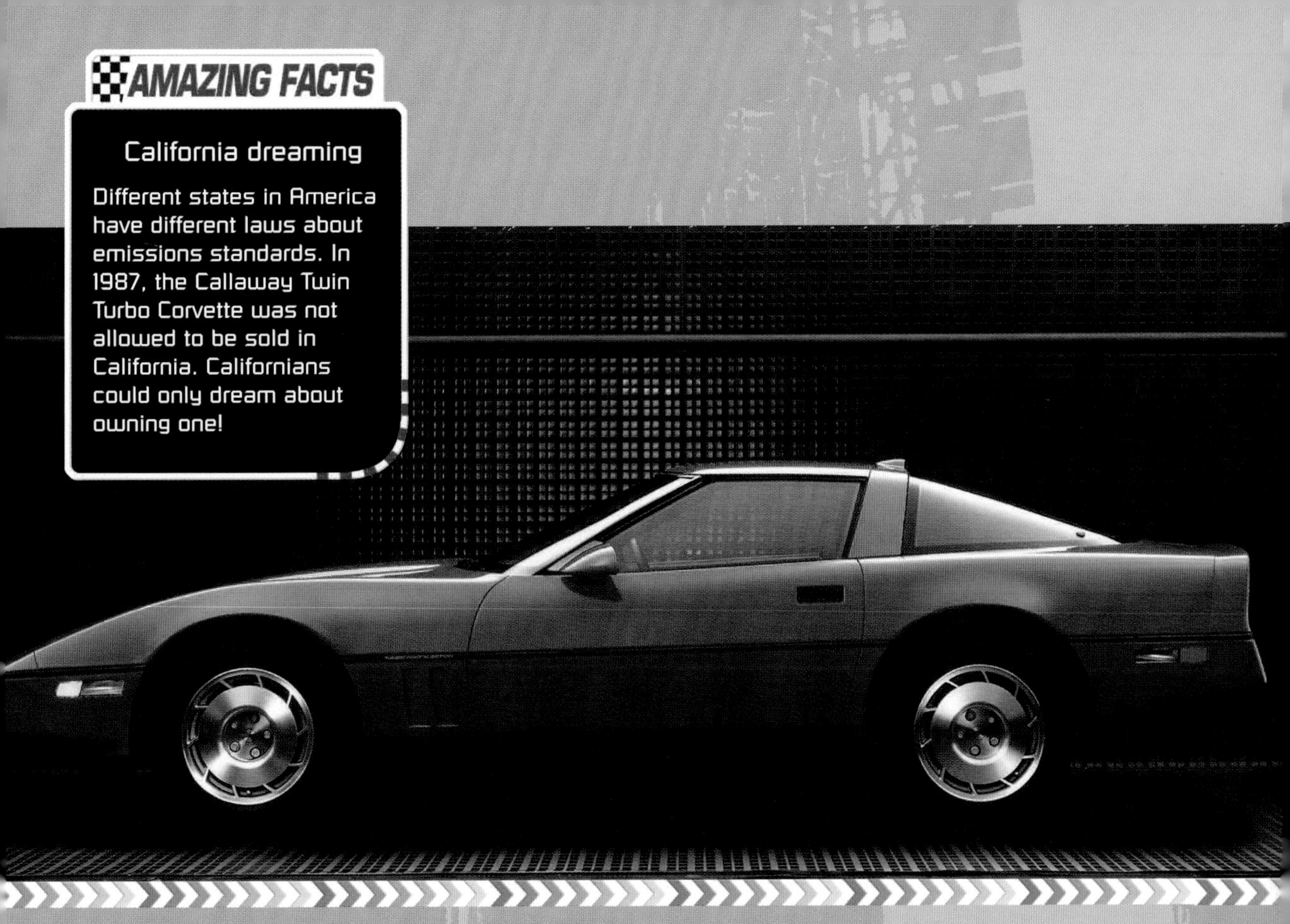

AMAZING FACTS

California dreaming

Different states in America have different laws about emissions standards. In 1987, the Callaway Twin Turbo Corvette was not allowed to be sold in California. Californians could only dream about owning one!

From 1987, turbocharged Corvettes were offered—they were sometimes referred to as Sledgehammers because they were so powerful.

More power

In 1987, the horsepower of the small-block V8 engine was boosted even more. The team designed new roller valve lifters that upped the horsepower from 230 (in the 1986 model) to 240. This was also the year that the Callaway Twin Turbo was installed in special-edition Corvettes. It was offered until the 1991 model. The cars were produced at Bowling Green and then shipped to Old Lyme, Connecticut, to have a turbocharger installed in the engine.

Turbocharging

A turbocharger compresses gas and shoots it into the engine to create more power. In this case it upped horsepower from 240 to an amazing 345! Top speed was around 177 mph (285 km/h). The Twin Turbo option came with a US$20,000 price tag. That means it would cost about US$37,000 today. And that's just the price of the option—a buyer would still have to pay around US$30,000 for the Corvette itself!

ZR-1

Production years: 1990–95
No. built: 6,939
Top speed: 180 mph (290 km/h)
Engine type: LT5
Engine size: 350 ci (5.7 liter), 375 hp
Cylinders: 8
Transmission: 6-speed manual
CO_2 emissions: 12.4 tons/yr
EPA fuel economy ratings: 16 mpg (city); 25 mpg (highway)
Price: US$64,138

Supercar ZR-1

The ZR-1 was supposed to come out in 1989, but it was fashionably late and was not released until a year later—in 1990. Buyers quickly forgave the company for the late delivery, despite the fact that this **supercar** had a super price tag of around US$60,000.

The ZR-1's LT-5 engine was an absolute powerhouse. It had been designed by Chevrolet and Lotus engineers. Lotus was a car company from England that specialized in designing racecars.

AMAZING FACTS

One million mark

The one millionth Corvette rolled off the assembly line at the plant in Bowling Green, Kentucky, on July 2, 1992. It was a white Corvette with a red interior—just like the very first Corvettes produced in 1953!

The fourth generation lasted 13 years – until 1997. It fell only one year short of the third generation, the longest-lived.

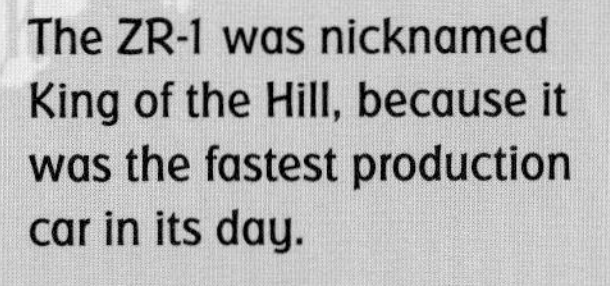

The ZR-1 was nicknamed King of the Hill, because it was the fastest production car in its day.

Fourth-generation facelift

The C4 Corvettes' looks were freshened up a bit for the 1990s, beginning with the 1991 model. All Corvettes were given the boxier-styled taillights that only the ZR-1 had the year before. Front bumpers were a bit more rounded. Side vent panels were horizontal instead of vertical.

New, too, were the fog and turning lights, which now wrapped around the front bumper. The black molding that split the car horizontally in half was replaced with the same body color molding instead. These small changes made a big difference in the overall appearance of the Corvette—but not enough to call it a new generation.

New millennium generation

GM released its fifth-generation (C5) Corvette in 1997. This time, different Corvette departments worked together to create the new car under one roof. These departments were marketing, design, engineering, and manufacturing. As a team, they created an entirely new chassis, engine, and body for the C5—something that no generation could ever brag about before. Many car magazines called it the best Corvette ever (but it was used to being called that by this time)!

Refined style

Stylewise, the fifth generation's overall look was much more rounded. The cars were "refined," which means perfected. The cars had a low hoodline that made it easier to see the road ahead. For the first time, the C5 Corvette unibody frame was made from a lightweight, **hydroformed** aluminum. Comfort improved, too, with the addition of a new floorboard design with a balsa-wood center surrounded by a glass-fiber material that reduced the car's noise and vibration.

The taillights on the 1997 Corvette—the first of the C5s—returned to a more rounded shape.

1997 Corvette

Production years: 1997
No. built: 9,752
Top speed: 172 mph (277 km/h)
Engine type: LS1 V8
Engine size: 350 ci (5.7 liter), 350 hp
Cylinders: 8
Transmission: Automatic (standard); 6-speed manual (optional)
CO_2 emissions: 9.8 tons/yr
EPA fuel economy ratings: 16 mpg (city); 24 mpg (highway)
Price: US$37,495

Flat tire? No problem

Even the tires on fifth-generation Corvettes were different. The front and rear tires were different diameters; 17 inches (43 cm) in the front and 18 inches (46 cm) in the rear. Plus, if one of these Goodyear Extended Mobility tires went flat, you could keep driving on it for up to a further 200 miles (320 km).

Under the hood

The C5's LS1 engine was still considered a small-block V8 but it had been almost completely redesigned. It was much lighter because it was made of aluminum instead of cast iron. It was smaller but more powerful than any previous small-block. Moving the transmission from under the hood to the back of the car made the back as heavy as the front and gave better balance overall.

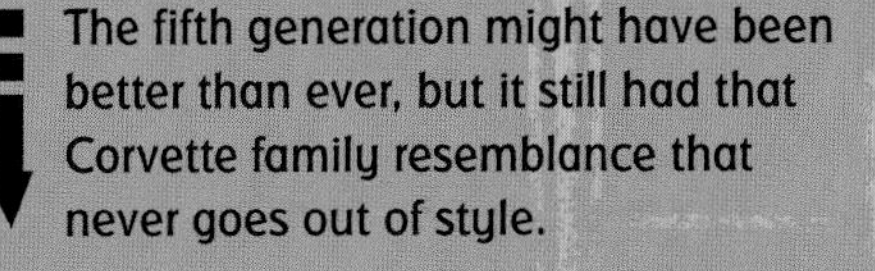
The fifth generation might have been better than ever, but it still had that Corvette family resemblance that never goes out of style.

ZO6

The name ZO6 had not been used for a Chevrolet Corvette since 1963. Back then, it was applied to the Sting Ray with a racing performance package. In 2001, the ZO6 was brought back to life.

On the outside it looked like a C5 Corvette but with the addition of brake-cooling mesh panels behind the bottom of the doors. Under the hood it had a high-performance LS6 engine that had 40 horsepower more than the standard LS1 engine.

Ending on a high

C5 Corvettes enjoyed an eight-year run. The special edition 2004 Le Mans ZO6 marked the final year of production for this generation. The special edition model was painted a blue metallic color with a silver racing stripe outlined in red. The colors honored Corvettes' first and second place wins at the 2001 24 Hours of Le Mans race, in the GTS (Grand Touring Sedan) class. The car was also given a carbon-fiber hood, which was stronger and lighter than fiberglass.

The new ZO6 had more effective racing performance than the Sting Ray had in 1963.

Corvette goes high-tech

For the first time ever, the 1999 Corvette could be outfitted with something called Heads-Up Display (HUD). With it, a Corvette driver can see speed or fuel-level information right on the windshield, just as the pilot of a fighter jet does. A projector in the instrument panel beams the image onto the windshield so the driver does not have to look away from the road.

The sixth generation

Corvettes are known for having state-of-the-art technology, style, and performance. To keep up this reputation, some of the greatest minds in the auto business continually push the limits of what can be added to the Corvette. That is why, in 2005, the sixth generation of Corvettes was released.

Smaller size

The GM design team, led by designer Tom Peters, made the sixth generation smaller than the fifth. The C6 was over five inches (13 cm) shorter and one inch (three cm) narrower. The C6 wheelbase increased by one inch (three cm) to give it a smoother ride. The design team looked at a jet fighter called the F22 Raptor to get ideas for designing the sixth-generation Corvette body.

The new smaller size, introduced in 2005 in the sixth-generation models, made the narrower European roads easier to drive.

One change in the C6 design was the introduction of exposed headlights to replace the traditional Corvette pop-ups.

C6 design features

For the first time in 42 years, a new Corvette generation does not have hidden headlights. Because the C6 does not need motors to pop the headlights up and down, it is lighter. Less weight also makes it more aerodynamic when the lights are on. There are no door handles on the C6 Corvette. Doors are opened with an electronic touch pad.

Engine power

The C6 Corvette was given a newly updated small-block V8 engine called the LS2. In 2005, it was the most powerful standard engine found in a Corvette. It had 400 hp and was even lighter than the LS1. Amazingly, the Corvette remained within the gas-tax standard, which meant that owners did not have to worry about paying extra taxes for their powerful cars.

Power up!

Just when drivers thought the Corvette couldn't possibly go any faster, GM created a bigger, better, lighter engine. The 2008 model Corvette had a new LS3 engine with 30 more horsepower than before, giving it a whopping 430 hp under the hood.

The 2008 model had an incredible new engine that gave it a top speed of 190 mph (306 km/h).

Z06 returns

The ZO6 model of Corvette came back in 2006 for round three. It has always been known as an extra-fast version of Corvette, and this car was no different. It was equipped with an even faster LS7 engine with 505 hp and a new six-speed automatic paddle-shifted transmission. The engine has parts made of a titanium **alloy**. Titanium is a silver metal that is lightweight and very strong, and does not break down easily. The frame of the car is made of aluminum, which makes it much lighter, too.

Vital Statistics

2008 Corvette

Production years: 2008
No. built: 35,310
Top speed: 190 mph (306 km/h)
Engine type: LS3 small-block V8
Engine size: 376 ci (6.2 liters), 430 hp
Cylinders: 8
Transmission: 6-speed manual; paddle-shift 6-speed automatic (optional)
CO_2 emissions: 9.8 tons/yr
EPA fuel economy ratings: 16 mpg (city); 26 mpg (highway)
Price: US$45,170 (coupe)

Chapter 5

Specialty Corvettes

Specialty Corvettes are the ones that you'll probably never see driving to the mall. These are the concept cars **that work out the kinks before a new generation goes into production. They're the cars that buzz around a racetrack for hours and hours, as in the 24 Hours of Le Mans endurance race. Or they're the cars that pace those races.**

A collection of Corvette concept cars from the 1960s to the 1990s. A concept car's design often exaggerates the characteristics of an actual production car.

Concept Corvettes

Many talented people's dreams, ideas, and hard work go into every new generation of Corvette. The very first ideas for a new generation begin as a concept car. A concept is something that takes form in a person's mind, like a thought or an idea. A concept car brings that idea one step closer to becoming a production car. Usually it is a one-of-a-kind car that designers and engineers can experiment with, to see what is good or bad about the idea.

XP-700

One of the first Corvette concept cars was the XP-700. XP stands for "experimental." This was Bill Mitchell's pet-project car. He took a 1958 Corvette and restyled it, making the nose of the car much longer, with curvy, raised front fenders, side indents, and a rounded rear end with two round taillights on each side. These features were seen again in the first of the second-generation Corvettes that came out in 1963. The car also had the split-window treatment that the 1963 Corvette had.

Sting Ray Racer

The first Sting Ray concept car, called the Sting Ray Racer, was designed by Bill Mitchell and Larry Shinoda in 1959. On the racetrack it was test-driven by Dr. Dick Thompson, a famous racecar driver (and dentist). It won the Sports Car Club of America (SCCA) National Racing Championship in 1960. The Sting Ray production car followed it in 1963.

Corvette now

Fifty years later, in 2009, another Corvette Stingray concept car was created. It is sometimes called the Corvette Centennial. It had some of the same styles used on the first Sting Ray Racer, such as the split back window. It is a design model only and is not equipped with any special technology or engine.

The Corvette Stingray concept car on display at the International Auto Show, in Chicago.

Mitchell's Makos

During his time at General Motors, Bill Mitchell was mainly interested in concept cars. He also enjoyed deep-sea fishing. This combination of hobbies explains why his ideas for future Corvettes included names such as the Mako Shark and, later, the Mako Shark II.

The sleek Mako Shark—one of Bill Mitchell's concept cars—on display in 1961, prior to its proper launch the following year.

Mako Shark

The Mako Shark first appeared in 1962. It looked like a shark from both a front and side profile. It was even painted to resemble the fierce fish, with dark blue on top that dissolved into a silvery white underbelly at the bottom. It had a mouthlike front grill, and three finlike gills on the front fenders. It also had four sidepipe exhausts that ran from behind the front fenders along the bottom of the doors.

AMAZING FACTS

Superstar cars

The first Sting Ray Racer concept car got a starring role in the 1957 Elvis Presley movie "Clambake." In the movie it was driven by Elvis himself. Fifty years later, the anniversary Stingray concept car was also given a starring role as "Sideswipe" in the movie "Transformers: The Revenge of the Fallen."

Mako Shark II

Bill Mitchell didn't stop at just one Mako, though. A few years later he began work on a refined model. The Mako Shark II was first shown as an experimental car in 1965. It featured all the new styling and technology that the designers and engineers at General Motors could dream of. With its curvy front and back fenders, it looked like the C3 Corvettes that were first released in 1968.

Aerovette

The Aerovette was a concept Corvette design that came out in 1974. This car had a four-rotor engine mounted in the middle of the car, instead of in the front. The mid-mounted rotary engine never made it to production Corvettes. GM decided to stick with the small-block V8s at the front of the car. Corvette designer Jerry Palmer took some design ideas from the Aerovette's less curvy styling when he created the 1984 Corvette.

The Aerovette featured gullwing doors that opened upward instead of sideways.

The CERV series

CERV I (Chevrolet Experimental Racing Vehicle) was a single-seat, mid-engine concept car created by Zora Arkus-Duntov in 1959. It was a racecar design with open wheels that were not under fenders. It did not look like a production Corvette!

CERV II was created in 1964 by Arkus-Duntov, with designers Larry Shinoda and Tom Lapine. It was a two-seater, with four-wheel drive and extremely curvy front and back fenders. It was given an all-aluminum V8 engine that could travel at speeds of 115 mph (185 km/h) and went from 0 to 60 mph (97 km/h) in four seconds. This concept car looked a lot more like the 1968 production Corvette than the CERV I.

First to the finish line

Where's the best place to test a fast sports car? On a racetrack, of course!

When Corvettes first came out in 1954, a professional racetrack was also one of the best places to advertise their superstardom. General Motors took full advantage of this, and entered its new V8 small-block 1955 Corvette at Pikes Peak in Colorado, where it set a new class record. Corvettes haven't stayed still since.

CERV III was built in 1985. It is sometimes called the Corvette Indy. It had a mid-mounted engine, an LT5 V8 that was of the type later used in the ZR1 Corvette.

Corvette began racing the 24 Hours of Le Mans in 1959. The car's racing career extends from that day to this.

AMA racing ban

In 1958, the Automobile Manufacturer's Association (AMA) put a ban on sponsoring the racing of production sports cars for large car companies like GM. The point was to encourage car buyers to purchase vehicles that were safe and reliable instead of fast. GM supported the ban, but racecar drivers still raced Corvettes—they just did it privately without the financial support of GM.

First 24 Hours of Le Mans

Corvettes were first raced on an international racetrack in France, at the 24 Hours of Le Mans endurance race in 1959. Of the three Corvettes that entered, only one lasted the full 24 hours and came in eighth place in its class.

Race-ready Sting Ray

In 1963, a Corvette Grand Sport with an aluminum-block V8 engine that put out 550 hp was planned—but was quickly canceled. GM executives were upset because they had supported the AMA's racing ban, and this car was clearly made for the racetrack. The assembly line had made five Grand Sport car bodies before they were canceled. Two men managed to get hold of two of these and later added Corvette engines to them. Dr. Dick Thompson raced one of these cars at Watkins Glen, New York, and took home first place. Even though GM was not allowed to race Corvettes under the AMA ban, others were winning races with them!

Corvettes are constantly being refined for racing. Here, a Corvette Z06 leads the field at the FIA GT race.

Secret Corvette racecars

In 1967, a Corvette could be purchased with a 560 hp big-block L88 engine. This vehicle was not made for the around-town driver—and would actually overheat if driven at highway speeds! But on the racetrack these L88-engine Corvettes were champions. They set record times and finished first in races such as the 12 Hours at Sebring in 1967.

The Corvette Challenge

In 1988, the Corvette was no longer able to compete at SCCA competitions. Instead, GM engineers created their own race called the Corvette Challenge. Only Corvettes were allowed to race. Corvette Challenge cars had to be ordered, and anyone wishing to buy one had to have a special Corvette Challenge license to even own one.

C5-R off to the races

The 1999 C5-R is a fifth-generation Corvette that was made specifically for racing. GM had not built such a car since the original AMA ban in 1957. The ban was long gone, but only in the 1990s did GM executives feel the time was right to reinstate a Corvette racing program. The C5-R brought home wins at races all around the world.

Next generation—C6-R

The sixth generation's answer to a sports-car racer was the C6-R. Again, it proved itself a first-class racing machine and brought home numerous first-place finishes in the 24 Hours of Le Mans and ALMS competitions. The C6-R was created for the racetrack and had a LS7R V8 engine.

Setting the pace

A pace car is a vehicle that slows racecars down if there is a caution period during a race. During caution periods, racecars cannot pass each other. When the pace car leaves the track, the race continues.

Throughout its history, Corvette has had the honor of pacing some very important races all around the world. Some (but not all) models of Corvette pace cars offer limited-edition lookalike pace cars for buyers. These may look like the pace car, but they do not have the **modified** engine.

Celebrity pace-car drivers

Who gets to drive some of these prestigious pace cars for the big races? Famous actors, politicians, racecar drivers, athletes, comedians, and talk-show hosts—that's who! Celebrity pace-car drivers have included General Colin Powell, Ashton Kutcher, Morgan Freeman, Jay Leno, and Lance Armstrong.

The official 2006 Z06 pace car that was driven by Jay Leno in the Indy 500. Pace cars have a specially modified engine to assist them on the track.

AMAZING FACTS

Going green

In 2008, Corvette created a different kind of concept car: a Z06 Corvette that runs on E85 ethanol fuel. Ethanol is a renewable alternative fuel that is made from crops grown in the United States. This environmentally friendly pace car was even painted Gold Rush Green.

The first Indy 500

In 1978, the twenty-fifth anniversary Corvette was the official pace car for the Indianapolis 500. It was the first Corvette ever to pace the track at Indianapolis. The pace-car edition Corvette was painted black on top and silver on the bottom. It had red-stripe detailing and came with special pace-car decals.

Late pace cars

In 2002, Corvette came back to pace the Indy 500 for its thirteenth time since 1978. The 2003 model used on this occasion celebrated the company's fiftieth anniversary. The deep glow of Red Xirallic crystal paint makes this Corvette really shine in the sunlight. Gold rippling-flag decals wrap around the hood and sides of the car. In 2008, Corvette's official pace car was a thirtieth-anniversary pace-car edition in the same colors as those the 1978 pace car came in: black and silver.

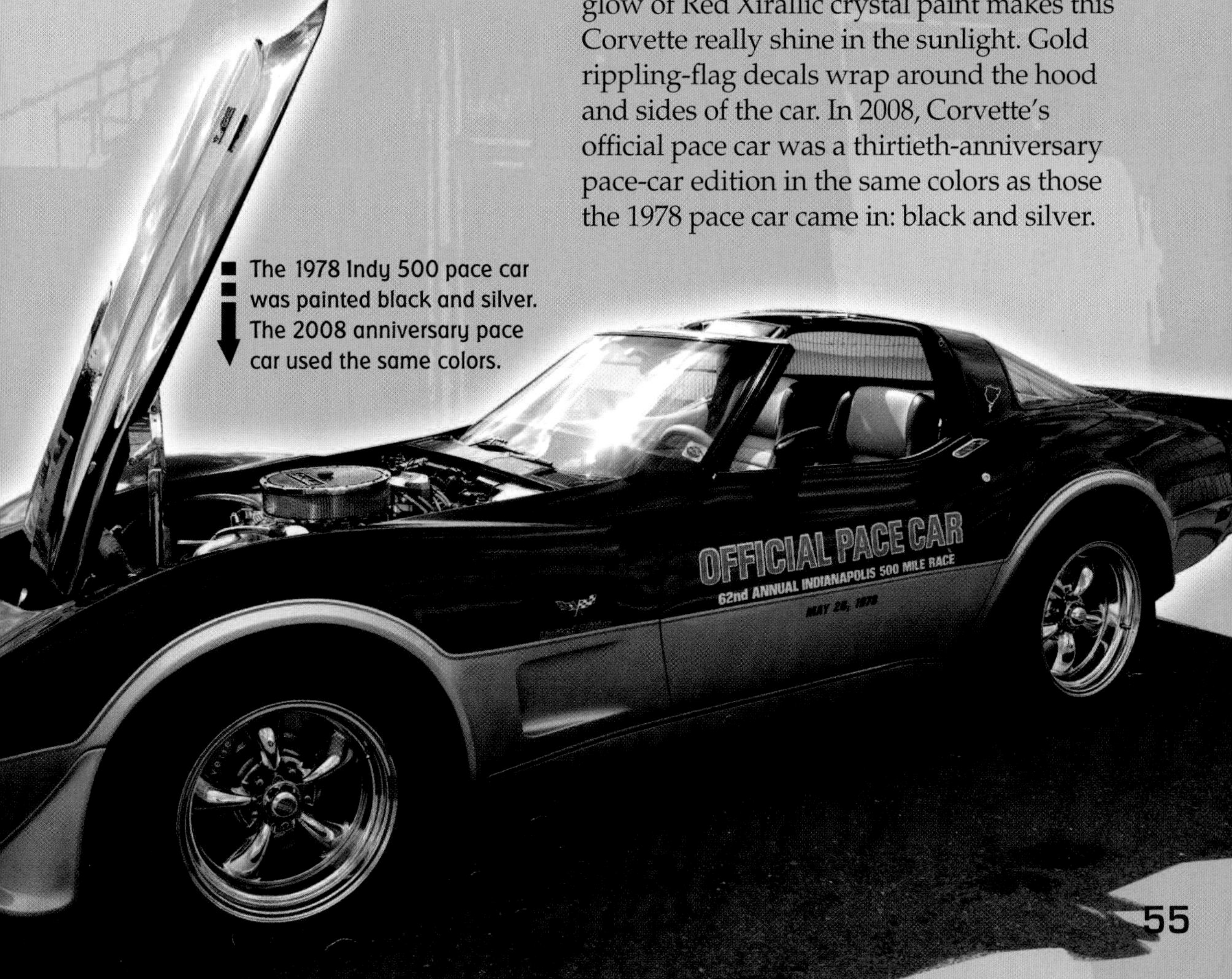

The 1978 Indy 500 pace car was painted black and silver. The 2008 anniversary pace car used the same colors.

Chapter 6

Driving Into the Future

It's not easy being America's favorite sports car. For over 50 years, Corvette has earned its reputation by pushing the limits of what can be done to improve the looks, comfort, and performance of its sports cars. The company has had to stay ahead of other American sports cars such as Pontiac's Trans Am, Dodge's Viper, and Ford's GT and Mustang. It's also had to keep up with foreign competitors such as Ferrari, Lamborghini, and Porsche.

The Kids Corvette Club

The Future Corvette Owners Association is a Corvette club for kids only. Those less than 16 years old are allowed to join as long as they are related to an adult member of the National Council of Corvette Clubs (NCCC). Members pay a one-time membership fee. Since the club was established in 1991, over 4,000 young Corvette lovers have joined.

Award-winning Corvettes

Car experts and magazine writers have given the Corvette praises and awards for its style, performance, and even price. *Motor Trend* magazine named the Corvette "Car of the Year" in 1984 and 1998. *Car and Driver* magazine's Reader's Choice Poll said the Corvette was the best all-around car nine times. *Automotive Engineering International* magazine awarded the 1999 Corvette the "Best Engineered Car of the 20th Century" award. In 2010, the American news magazine *U.S. News and World Report* chose the Corvette as the "Best Luxury Sports Car for the Money."

National Corvette Museum

The National Corvette Museum is the museum that Corvette lovers built. It opened on September 2, 1994, in Bowling Green, Kentucky—where all Corvettes are made. Different Corvette clubs, including the National Corvette Restorers Society and the National Council of Corvette Clubs, raised the money for the museum. Corporations such as GM, Mobile, Mid America Motorworks, and Goodyear gave their support to the project. The museum sells memberships to help keep it open. Over 35,000 Corvette lovers belong.

Displayed inside the large museum are many Corvette racecars and production models. Some are loaned and are there for only a certain amount of time. Others are donated to the museum for permanent display. There is even an area where Corvette owners can bring their own cars to be cleaned and later displayed!

The characteristic beauty, style, and performance of Corvettes have been winning awards for decades.

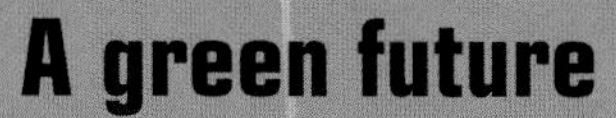

A green future

Corvettes are known for having state-of-the-art design and technology. The future of car making is leaning toward cars with "greener" engines. That is, cars are being equipped with alternatively powered engines that run on electricity or fuels other than gasoline. Some sports-car companies, such as Porsche, have **hybrid** engines that run on electricity and ethanol-based fuels. But Corvette doesn't have one for buyers—yet.

Vital Statistics

2010 Grand Sport Coupe

Production years: 2010
No. built: Still in production
Top speed: 186 mph (300 km/h)
Engine type: LS3 V8
Engine size: 376 ci (6.2 liter), 430 hp
Cylinders: 8
Transmission: 6-speed manual; 6-speed paddle-shift automatic (optional)
CO_2 emissions: 9.8 tons/yr
EPA fuel economy ratings: 16 mpg (city); 26 mpg (highway)
Price: US$55,720

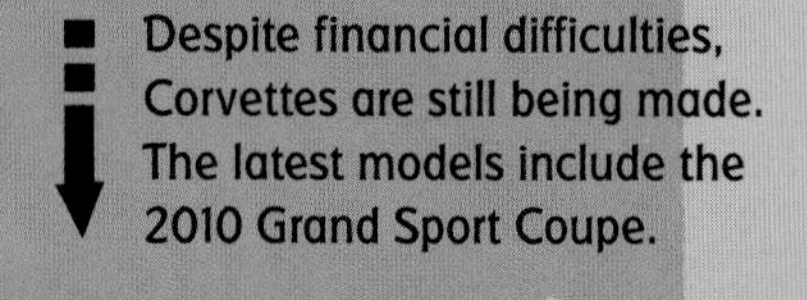

Despite financial difficulties, Corvettes are still being made. The latest models include the 2010 Grand Sport Coupe.

Corvettes never go out of style. Each design remains beautiful to look at, and each car's performance has made it one of the fastest American production sports cars ever.

Corvette continues...

Many drivers today rate Corvettes number one for style, performance, luxury, and especially affordability. These attributes have made it and kept it the leading sports car made in America. The popularity of Corvettes among sports-car lovers is a phenomenon that extends across America and all around the world.

America's favorite sports car gets better every year. Rumor has it that in 2013 the seventh-generation Corvette will be released. Whatever surprises this Corvette might have can only be guessed at. But given the car's track record, it will be beautiful to look at, comfortable to ride in, and very fast—all at an affordable price.

Financial crisis

The past few years have been troubled times for GM. The company suffered a financial crisis. In 2009, it filed for ***bankruptcy***. Various U.S. and Canadian government agencies invested billions of dollars in GM to help it survive. In 2009, GM closed its Pontiac division, sold Hummer to China, and sold off other brands to make up for losses. Chevrolet continues to make the Corvette and several other cars.

Corvette Timeline

1953	First Corvettes roll off the production line in Flint, Michigan
1954	Production moves to St. Louis; Corvettes are offered in a choice of four colors
1956	New-look Corvette is revealed
1957	First fuel-injected Corvette engine is used
1958	Corvette adopts chrome detailing; AMA bans large companies from race sponsorship
1959	First Sting Ray concept car is unveiled; Corvette races in its first 24 Hours of Le Mans
1962	The 1962 Corvette marks the last of the first generation; Mako Shark concept cars begin
1963	The Sting Ray is launched, with numerous design changes; Clean Air Act is introduced
1964	CERV II concept car is created
1965	Big-block engine option is offered in the Corvette
1967	L88 engine first offered in the Corvette
1968	Start of the third generation of Corvettes
1969	Sting Ray name becomes Stingray
1973	Chrome details start to be phased out in favor of urethane plastic
1974	Aerovette concept car is unveiled
1975	Corvette starts building all its cars with a catalytic converter
1978	Corvette celebrates its 25th anniversary; makes first appearance as pace car in the Indy 500
1983	The first of the fourth-generation Corvettes is launched—the 1984
1984	Sales of Corvettes reach an almost-record high
1987	Twin Turbo Callaway special edition is released
1990	Launch of the ZR-1 Corvette supercar
1992	The one millionth Corvette rolls off the production line
1997	First of the C5 Corvettes is revealed
1999	HUD is introduced as a feature in Corvettes
2001	New-model ZO6 is launched; Corvette places first and second in the 24 Hours of Le Mans race
2004	Special edition Le Mans ZO6 marks the end of the C5s
2005	Sixth-generation Corvettes begin
2006	ZO6 model is revived in a superfast update
2008	LS3 engine gives the 2008 model more power than ever before; green pace car is created for the Indy 500
2009	New Stingray concept car is displayed
2010	Grand Sport Coupe returns for 2010

Further Information

Books

Corvette: America's Top Sports Car
by Jerry Burton
(Lauter Levin Associates, Inc., 2006)

Corvette Black Book
by Mike Antonick
(Michael Bruce Associates Inc., 2010)

The Complete Book of Corvette
by Mike Mueller
(Motorbooks, 2006)

Web sites

www.chevrolet.com/corvette/
The official web site of the Chevrolet division of General Motors

www.corvetteclubofamerica.org/
The online home of the world's oldest Corvette Club

www.corvettemuseum.com/
The web site of the National Corvette Museum

Glossary

aerodynamic Describing a shape that is designed to move easily through wind at high speed

alloy A substance consisting of two or more metals or of a metal and a nonmetal combined

automatic transmission A device that shifts a car's gears without help from the driver according to the speed the car is traveling

bankruptcy The reduction of a company or individual to a state of impoverishment

catalytic converter A device attached to a car's exhaust system that makes its emissions less harmful

chassis The frame of a car

concept car A vehicle made to show the public a new design or technology

coupe A hard-topped sports car with two seats

coves Inwardly curved sections located behind the front wheel fender and door area on a Corvette

drag The force that slows down a moving body; the car moves in one direction against the air, which is moving in the opposite direction

embargo A governmental law that forbids trade with a specific country

emissions Substances that escape into the air from a vehicle's exhaust

exports Goods that are transported abroad for sale or trade

horsepower (hp) The amount of pulling power an engine has, calculated as the number of horses it would take to pull the same load

hybrid A car that uses both a regular combustion engine and an electric system

hydroformed Created by a process that shapes aluminum by injecting it with a fluid under high pressure; the end result is a frame that is lightweight and very strong

manual transmission A driver-operated device to shift a car's gears

maverick A strong-minded, independent, often unconventional individual

modified Changed, though not in a radical or fundamental way

muscle car A high-performance two-door car with a big, beefy engine

production car A car that is made in large numbers on an assembly line

recessed Set back from, indented

recession A period of time when the economy is not doing well

retractable Able to be withdrawn or concealed

roadster A two-seat car that has no roof or side windows

sedan A passenger car with four doors and a back seat

signature A distinctive and original characteristic or identifying mark

state-of-the-art Referring to the highest level of development at a given time

supercar An extremely fast, powerful, eye-catching sports car

urethane plastic A type of plastic that is especially tough and is often used as a protective coating

whitewall tires Tires with a circular band made of white rubber, popular in the 1950s and 1960s

Index

Entries in **bold** indicate pictures